Valuable Stamps Of China

THEODORE T. TSAVOUSSIS

ISBN:**1499702795**

ISBN-13:**978-1499702798**

DEDICATION

This book is dedicated to all philatelic hobbyists, young and old.

CONTENTS

VF	VERY FINE
HR	HINGE REMANANT
NG	NO GUM
PERF	PERFORTION SIZE
CAT	CATALOGUE
INV	INVERTED CENTER OR SURCHARGE
IMPERF	IMPERFECT (NO PERFORATIONS)
PRICE	ESTIMATE OF PRICE IN US DOLLARS

ACKNOWLEDGMENTS

The world of stamp collecting,
auctioning and selling of Rare stamps has seen some decline in the past few years. It is our
intention to bring back this once dying hobby.

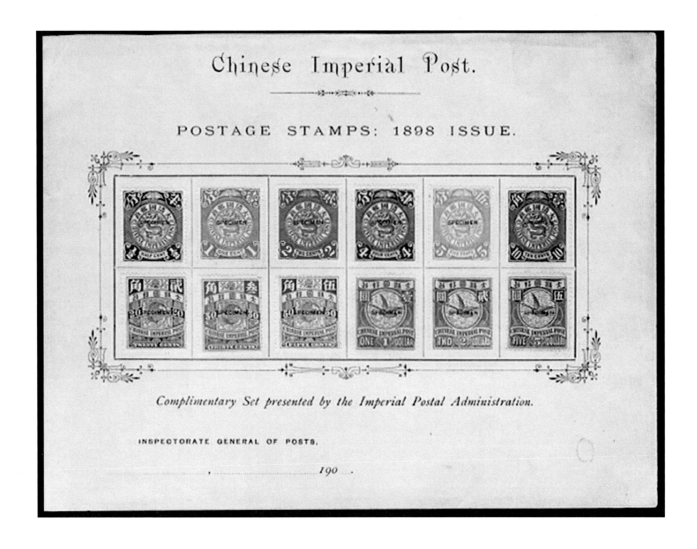

CHINA 1898 1/2c-$5 complete set of 12, each overprinted "Specimen" in small letters and mounted on an Imperial   Postal Administration presentation sheet, fine-v.f.

Price $1600.00 approx. US Dollars.

CHINA - PRC 1951 Gate of Heavenly Peace, Fifth Issue, $10,000-$200,000, complete set of six, unused without gum as issued, n.h., fine-v.f.,

Cat.   #95-100
Val. $5,637

Price $4000.00

CHINA - PRC 1953 Russian October Revolution, unissued set of four in different colors with additional "Soviet" characters, used, usual small faults, fine-v.f. appearance. A small number of these sets were unofficially released in Hunan, Fukien and Canton in February 1953,

Cat. #194-197var
Val. $8,000

Price $5500.00 approx.

CHINA - PRC 1962 Mai Lan-fang souvenir sheet, n.h. and post office fresh, few natural and minor wrinkles, v.f., truly close to perfect quality for this notoriously difficult sheet, signed Roumet, with his 2001 cert.,

.

Cat.   #628
Val. $12,000.00

Price $16000.00 approx

8

CHINA - PRC 1964 Peonies souvenir. sheet, unused without gum as issued, n.h., v.f.,

Cat. #782
Val. $3,000

CHINA - PRC 1964 15th Anniversary of the People's Republic souvenir sheet, n.h., few trivial gum wrinkles, still v.f.,

Cat.   #798a
Val. $3,200 .00

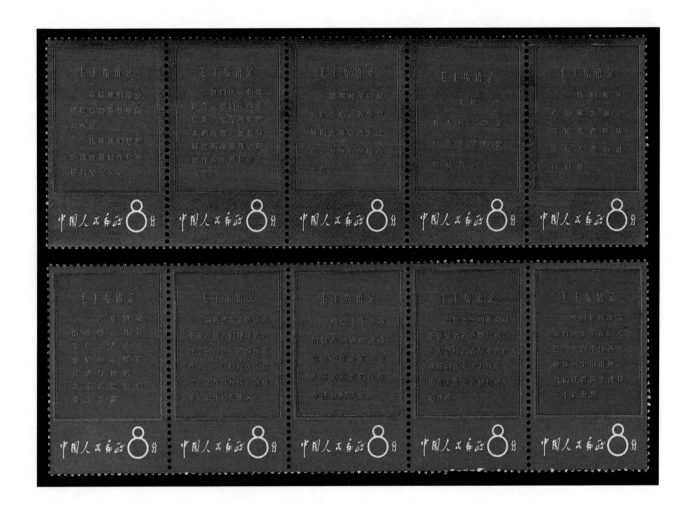

CHINA - PRC 1967 Thoughts of Mao, se-tenant strips of five, set of two, folded between stamps, h.r. fresh and v.f.,

Cat. #943a,948a
Val. $2,400

CHINA - PRC 1967-68 Poems by Mao, complete set, n.h., slight offsets on reverse, fine-v.f.,

Cat. #967-
80
Val. $3,085

CHINA - PRC 1968 Directives of Chairman Mao, unfolded horizontal strip of five, n.h. and post office fresh, one stamp with natural gum inclusion, v.f., one of the key items from the Cultural Revolution,

Cat.   #996a
Val. $4,500

The Whole Country Is Red

"The Entire Nation is Red", tiny postmark at lower left, with most of the gum still intact, minor mended perforations at right and wrinkles, still a v.f. example of this popular rarity,

Price $26,000.00

China - PRC

1958 8f rose lilac, incorrectly inscribed "5th Congress of World Students' Representatives" instead of "International Students' Union, 5th Congress", unused without gum as issued
Price : $9,200.00

China
1897 Red Revenues, $5 on 3c

(Scott   85)
Price: $17,250.00

CHINA 1896 unsurcharged Red Revenue stamp, 3c red, perforated 14, never hinged, few gum skips, post office fresh, v.f. and beautiful copy, with 2007 Experts and Consultants Ltd certificate. Originally ordered for internal use by the Customs Department, the 3c stamp inscribed "China" and "Revenue" was ordered from the London printing company Waterlow & Sons, following a request from Sir Robert Hart, the Inspector General of the Imperial Maritime Customs to James Campbell, the Customs Commissioner in London. The stamps were perforated 12 to 16 on three different machines and were shipped to China on 18th September, 1896. Although the stamps never served their intended purpose, they were pressed into use for surcharging in order to fulfill demand for stamps in the silver currency adapted by the newly inaugurated national postal system. Practically all of the 650,000 stamps ordered from London were used for this purpose, although there remained 761 stamps without surcharge stored at the General Post Office. During

Cat. #Chan R1

Price
$130,000.00

CHINA 1915 Hall of Classics First Peking Printing $2 black and blue, variety center inverted, bright colors, well centered for this, with vertical guideline at right, previously hinged, lightly hinged, very fine and fresh unused, with certificate (Chan 245a). Only one sheet of 50 of this variety was sold at the Hankow post office. One of the "Four Treasures of the Republic," ex-Denison collection (China Stamp Society Specialized Catalogue 277a, $275,000)

Cat. #237a   **Price**

Val. $172,500   **$160,000.00**

CHINA 1923 surcharged in red on first Peking printing 2 Cts on 3c blue-green, surcharge inverted error, deep bright color, characteristic centering to lower right, nevertheless well centered, very fine and fresh with original customary flat and streaky, h.r., signed Holcombe, Champion, with certificate (Chan 280a). It is believed that there are less than twenty examples known of this error. According to contemporary reports (Theodore Sidall), on thirteen of these stamps exist and were acquired at Wanhsien, a small port about half way between Chungking and Ichang, in July, 1924, by Dr. A. Germain, the medical officer on the French gunboat "Balny." He applied two of the stamps to separate covers which he mailed to himself locally and sold ten mint examples to the French dealer Theodore Champion. Champion than sold a block of four and a single to M.D. Chow, two singles to Bush and one each to Hinds and Hawkins. One of the "Four Treasures of the Republic," ex-H.G. Fletcher, S.Beckeman collections (China Stamp Soci

Cat. #247a
Val. $200,000

Price Approx
$170,000.00

China
1925 surcharged in red on second Peking printing 3 Cts on 4c slate-gray, surcharge inverted
error, used
Price : $276,000.00

China
1941 Dr. Sun Yat-sen New York Print $2 black and blue, variety center inverted
Price : $120,750.00

China - P.R.C.
1952 8f orange Tien An Men, unissued stamp with backing rays of Sunlight, used
Price $18,400.00

CHINA - PRC China - Soviet Republic Postage Dues 1932 1c yellow, horizontal imperf. pair, unused without gum as issued, v.f., with China National Postage Stamp Museum cert. (Yang SPD1a)

Cat. #SG	Price
SRD8var	$5,500.00

CHINA SHANGHAI Postage Dues 1893 2c-20c, imperforate Plate Essays on thick watermarked paper (Livingston D16EP-20EP), matching left margin horizontal pairs, each showing normal top left "screw head", se-tenant with "filled screw head" varieties, v.f. and rare set of five (essays in this format are not known for 1/2c and 1c values)

Cat. #J16-20E

Price
$4,500.00

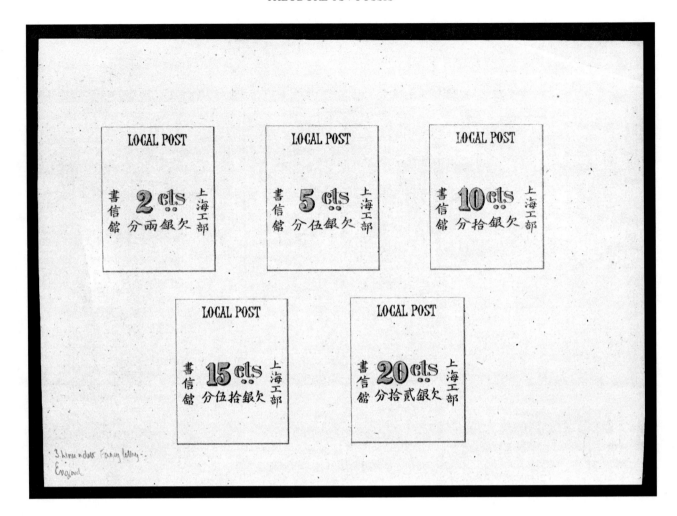

CHINA SHANGHAI Postage Dues 1893 Engraved die proof for the Numeral Issue, Barclay & Fray, London, composite die proof of five, essay for the inscription and value tablets in black, on glazed unsurfaced paper (lettering in fancy type and three lines of shading in dots), showing error in Chinese value "1 ct" for 2 cts, and lower character at left, corner crease, otherwise v.f., with Holcombe cert. A rare proof

Cat. #J16/20E

Price
$2,300.00

CHINA - PRC 1961 Table Tennis, five souvenir sheets, unused without gum as issued, one l.h., others n.h., some wrinkles, inclusions, light creases or minor stains, otherwise fine-v.f.

Cat. #566a
Val. $5,000

Price
$4,250.00

CHINA - PRC 1980 Monkey, corner margin block of four, n.h., faint natural black offsets of reverse, v.f.,   Cat. #1586   **Price**
Val. $4,000   **$4,000.00**

CHINA - PRC 1980 8f Monkey, irregular block of nine, used on cover from Peking   Cat. #1586   **Price**
to Germany, v.f. (catalogue value for used singles)   Val. $2,250   **$5,560.00**

CHINA - PRC Military Mail 1953 $800 yellow, orange & red, and $800 deep purple, orange & red, unused without gum, fine-v.f.

Cat. #M1-2

Price
$1,200.00

CHINA Formosa 1888 Horse & Dragon, 10c on 20 Cash green, red handstamp with frame, black handwriting, excellent color and centering, fine and very rare stamp

Cat. #Chan F21   Price $2400.00

CHINA 1897 $1 on 3r red, nearly perfect centering, fresh original white gum, h.r., v.f.,

Cat. #84
Val. $9,000

CHINA 1950 $1-$20 surcharges set of five, unused without gum as issued, fresh and v.f.

Cat. #1007-11   Price $7500.00

CHINA Special Delivery 1905 10c grass-green, unsevered strip of four (folded between stamps in the middle), perforated 11, Dragon's head facing downward, serial no. 930, unused, v.f., very rare,

Cat. #E1   **Price**
Val. $12,000   **$7,000.00**

German Colonies Offices in China
1900 Tientsin Issue, 50pf purple and black red, Mi. 13, SC. 22, cat. €20,000
Price $17,250.00

ABOUT THE AUTHOR

Theodore Tsavoussis is an avid stamp collector and a member of many Auction Houses worldwide. His knowledge of Rare Stamps was gathered from his late uncle Elefterios Tsavoussis.

Made in United States
North Haven, CT
09 June 2023

37509379R00024